...urned or ...r before
...ate :

Poems for Christmas

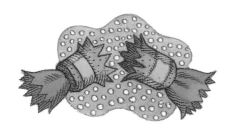

Poems for Christmas

Illustrated by Ian Beck ✷ Compiled by Jill Bennett

For
Patrick O'Connor

Scholastic Children's Books
Commonwealth House, 1-19 New Oxford Street
London WC1A 1NU, UK
a division of Scholastic Ltd
London ~ New York ~ Toronto ~ Sydney ~ Auckland
Mexico City ~ New Delhi ~ Hong Kong

First published in hardback in the UK by Scholastic Publications Ltd, 1992
First published in paperback in the UK by Scholastic Ltd, 1993
Revised paperback edition first published in the UK by Scholastic Ltd, 1999
This revised paperback edition first published in the UK by Scholastic Ltd, 2003

Selection, arrangement and editorial matter © Jill Bennett and Scholastic Ltd, 1992
Illustrations copyright © Ian Beck, 1992

ISBN 0 439 97783 5

Printed by Proost, Belgium

2 4 6 8 10 9 7 5 3 1

Contents

ACKNOWLEDGEMENTS

The editor and publisher are grateful for permission to include the following copyright material in this anthology:

Rodney Bennett, "Ten Little Christmas Trees", from *Seeing and Doing Book* (Thames TV), © Rodney Bennett.

Gerard Benson, "Lullaby Carol" was first written for a Nativity Play at Ring Cross Infants' School and is reprinted by permission of the author.

Jacqueline Brown, "Christmas Story" © Jacqueline Brown, 1968. Reprinted by permission of the author.

Charles Causley, "High in the Heaven" from *The Gift of a Lamb* (Robson Books). Reprinted by permission of David Higham Associates Ltd.

Sue Cowling, "Country Carol" from *What is a Kumquat?* Reprinted by permission of Faber & Faber Ltd.

Richard Edwards, "Pilot" from *If Only* © Richard Edwards, 1990. First published by Viking Kestrel. Reprinted by permission of Penguin Books Ltd, and Felicity Bryan, Literary Agent.

Aileen Fisher, "Christmas Secrets" from *Out in the Dark and Daylight* © Aileen Fisher, 1970. Reprinted by permission of the author.

Jean Kenward, "Sir Winter". Reprinted by permission of the author.

Adrian Mitchell, "Mrs Christmas" from *All My Own Stuff* (Simon & Schuster Ltd). Reprinted with permission of the Peters, Fraser & Dunlop Group Ltd.

John Mole, "The Waiting Game" from *Catching the Spider* (Blackie, 1990), © John Mole, 1990.

Charles Williams, "Kings Came Riding", first published in *Modern Verse for Little Children* (OUP, 1927). Reprinted by permission of David Higham Associates Ltd.

Little Jack Horner

Little Jack Horner
Sat in the corner
Eating his Christmas pie.
He put in his thumb
And pulled out a plum
And said, "What a good boy am I."

anon.

Country Carol

Walked on the crusted grass in the frosty air.
Blackbird saw me, gave me a gold-rimmed stare.

Walked in the winter woods where the snow lay deep.
Hedgehog heard me, smiled at me in his sleep.

Walked by the frozen pond where the ice shone pale.
Wind sang softly, moon dipped its silver sail.

Walked on the midnight hills till the star-filled dawn.
No one told me, I knew a king was born.

Sue Cowling

The Waiting Game

Nuts and marbles in the toe,
An orange in the heel,
A Christmas stocking in the dark
Is wonderful to feel.

Shadowy, bulging length of leg
That crackles when you clutch,
A Christmas stocking in the dark
Is marvellous to touch.

You lie back on your pillow
But that shape's still hanging there.
A Christmas stocking in the dark
Is very hard to bear.

So try to get to sleep again
And chase the hours away.
A Christmas stocking in the dark
Must wait for Christmas Day.

John Mole

Christmas Secrets

Secrets long and secrets wide,
brightly wrapped and tightly tied,

Secrets fat and secrets thin,
boxed and sealed and hidden in,

Some that rattle, some that squeak,
some that caution "Do Not Peek" . . .

Hurry, Christmas, get here first,
get here fast . . . before we *burst*.

Aileen Fisher

In the Bleak Midwinter

In the bleak midwinter
Frosty wind made moan;
Earth stood hard as iron,
Water like a stone;
Snow had fallen, snow on snow,
Snow on snow,
In the bleak midwinter,
Long ago.

Our God, heaven can not hold him
Nor earth sustain;
Heaven and earth shall flee away
When he comes to reign;
In the bleak midwinter
A stable place sufficed
The Lord God almighty,
Jesus Christ.

What can I give him,
Poor as I am?
If I were a shepherd
I would bring a lamb;
If I were a wise man
I would do my part;
Yet what can I give him –
Give my heart.

Christina Rossetti

Mrs Christmas

She was about as small as a cup
But big as your head when she grew up
And she came to stay on Christmas Day
So we called her Mrs Christmas

She liked to swoop around the hall
With a silver paper soccer ball
And I think I was four but maybe some more
When I named her Mrs Christmas

She had some kittens with bright white socks
And she kept them in a brown cardboard box
And she'd nudge them out and march them about
Saying: "I am Mrs Christmas".

Adrian Mitchell

Pilot

If I could be a pilot
Each Christmas Eve I'd fly
To fetch a fluffy snow cloud
From the distant Arctic sky,
I'd chase it, catch it, tow it home
And tie it to a tree,
So snow would fall on Christmas Day
On all my friends and me.

Richard Edwards

Lullaby Carol

Mary sang to her pretty baby
Sleep, little one, sleep,
And all the bright angels
Of heaven sang with her
Sleep, little one, sleep.

Some shepherds heard them in the fields
Where they were watching their sheep,
They went to the stable
And joined in the carol
Sleep, little one, sleep.

From faraway lands came kings
Over the mountains so steep,
With gifts for the baby
They joined in the carol
Sleep, little one, sleep.

Sleep, little one, sleep,
Close your eyes and don't peep,
Your father and mother
Are watching your cradle
Sleep, little one, sleep.

Gerard Benson

The Snow Lies White

The snow lies white on roof and tree,
  Frost fairies creep about,
The world's as still as it can be,
  And Santa Claus is out.

He's making haste his gifts to leave,
  While the stars show his way,
There'll soon be no more Christmas Eve,
  Tomorrow's Christmas Day!

anon.

Kings came riding

Kings came riding
   One, two and three,
Over the desert
   And over the sea.

One in a ship
   With a silver mast;
The fishermen wondered
   As he went past.

One on a horse
   With a saddle of gold;
The children came running
   To behold.

One came walking,
   Over the sand,
With a casket of treasure
   Held in his hand.

All the people
   Said, "where go they?"
But the kings went forward
   All through the day.

Night came on
   As those kings went by;
They shone like the gleaming
   Stars in the sky.

Charles Williams

Sir Winter

I heard Sir Winter coming.
He crept out of his bed
and rubbed his thin and freezing hands:
"I'll soon be up!" he said.

"I'll shudder at the keyhole
and rattle at the door,
I'll strip the trees of all their leaves
and strew them on the floor.

"I'll harden every puddle
that Autumn thinks is his –
I'll lay a sparkling quilt of snow
on everything that is!

"I'll bring a load of darkness
as large as any coal,
and drive my husky dogs across
the world, from pole to pole.

"Oho! How you will shiver!"
– And then I heard him say;
"But in the middle of it all
I'll give you

　　　　CHRISTMAS DAY!"

Jean Kenward

The Christmas Pudding

Into the basin
put the plums,
Stir-about, stir-about,
stir-about!

Next the good
white flour comes,
Stir-about, stir-about,
stir-about!

Sugar and peel
and eggs and spice,
Stir-about, stir-about,
stir-about!

Mix them and fix them
and cook them twice,
Stir-about, stir-about,
stir-about!

anon.

An Old Christmas Greeting

Sing hey!
Sing hey!
For Christmas Day;
Twine mistletoe and holly.
For friendship glows
In winter snows,
And so let's all be jolly!

anon.

Ten Little Christmas Trees

Ten little Christmas trees
  a-growing in a line.
The first went to Bedfordshire.
  And that left only nine.

Nine little Christmas trees
  all found it long to wait.
The second went to Monmouthshire,
  And that left only eight.

Eight little Christmas trees said,
  "Christmas will be heaven."
The third went to London Town,
  And that left only seven.

Seven little Christmas trees,
  and all as straight as sticks!
The fourth went to Oxfordshire,
  And that left only six.

Six little Christmas trees,
  all growing and alive!
The fifth went to Lancashire,
  And that left only five.

Five little Christmas trees said,
  "Will they want some more?"
The sixth went to Devonshire,
  And that left only four.

Four little Christmas trees,
  as sturdy as could be!
The seventh went to Scilly Isles,
  And that left only three.

Three little Christmas trees
  all grew up and grew and grew,
the eighth went to Middlesex,
  And that left only two.

Two little Christmas trees,
  December almost done!
The ninth went to Timbuktu,
  And that left only one.

One little Christmas tree,
  feeling very small!
She came to our school,
  And that was best of all.

Ten little Christmas trees,
  with Christmas drawing near,
Wish you love and gladness,
  And a Happy New Year.

Rodney Bennett

Christmas Story

Shepherds, wakeful, weary,
On bare hillsides stony,
In the midnight clearly
Hear the angels' story.

Star, jewel-bright, lovely,
Above a stable lowly,
Wherein a maiden, Mary,
Tends a baby gently.

Wise men, rich and mighty,
To Bethlehem ride slowly
To offer presents costly,
Honour the birth of a baby.

In the warm manger, safely,
Christ, the child, sleeps soundly –
To all the poor and lonely
God's gift once only.

Jacqueline Brown

High in the Heaven

High in the Heaven
A gold star burns
Lighting our way
As the great world turns.

Silver the frost
It shines on the stem.
As we now journey
To Bethlehem.

White is the ice
At our feet as we tread,
Pointing a path
To the manger-bed.

Charles Causley